Depressio
AND
beyond

A GUIDE TO PATTERN IDENTIFICATION

Doris Yeske

Schiffer Publishing Ltd

4880 Lower Valley Road, Atglen, PA 19310 USA

Dedication

To my loyal and supportive friends, members of the antique club "Tickled By Time," and Erv Bringe, manager of the antique mall in West Salem, Wisconsin. Without their encouragement, enthusiasm, and assistance in every aspect—especially in locating the numerous patterns of glassware—this third book would not have been completed. This book has been a challenge and I truly appreciate their immense support.

Copyright © 2003 by Doris Yeske
Library of Congress Control Number: 2002115870

Designed by Bonnie M. Hensley
Cover design by Bruce M. Waters
Type set in Zapf Calligraphy BT/Korinna BT

ISBN: 0-7643-1759-8
Printed in China
1 2 3 4

Published by Schiffer Publishing Ltd.
4880 Lower Valley Road
Atglen, PA 19310
Phone: (610) 593-1777; Fax: (610) 593-2002
E-mail: Schifferbk@aol.com
Please visit our web site catalog at **www.schifferbooks.com**
We are always looking for people to write books on new and related subjects. If you have an idea for a book, please contact us at the above address.

This book may be purchased from the publisher.
Include $3.95 for shipping.
Please try your bookstore first.
You may write for a free catalog.

In Europe, Schiffer books are distributed by
Bushwood Books
6 Marksbury Avenue
Kew Gardens
Surrey TW9 4JF England
Phone: 44 (0) 20 8392 8585
Fax: 44 (0) 20 8392 9876
E-mail: Bushwd@aol.com
Free postage in the UK. Europe: air mail at cost.

Contents

Preface

This book focuses on the classification and identification of Depression Glass and other collectible glassware by the prominent design in the pattern. To better assist collectors, non-collectors, and dealers, I have classified the patterns into design categories, each with the names of the associated patterns in alphabetical order. It is my hope that this type of reference guide will be extremely useful in assisting anyone interested in identifying and collecting glassware.

1. Animals

Fire King – "Game Bird," Anchor Hocking Glass Corp. 1959-1962. An anchor white pattern with the motif of a bird labeled Ruffled Grouse.
Colors: white with decal

Mug, 8oz., $8.

Fontaine, Tiffin Glass Co. 1924-1931. This pattern has an etched design of birds at an ornate water fountain.
Colors: crystal with green, pink, twilight, twilight with crystal, and crystal with amber

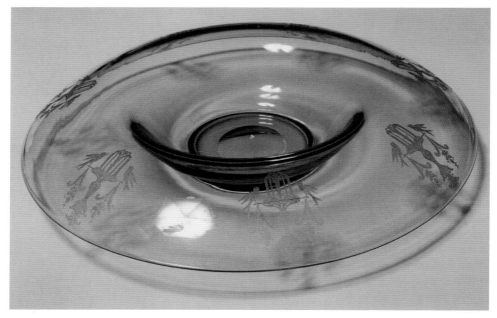

Bowl, reversible, $55.

Georgian, "Lovebirds," Federal Glass Co. 1931-1936. Very unique pattern with two lovebirds (parakeets) perched side by side with alternating baskets.
  Colors: green, crystal, and amber

Creamer, $12; Sugar, $10.

Bowl, 5-3/4" cereal, $25; Plate, luncheon, $11; Bowl, 4-1/2" berry, $9.

Parrot, "Sylvan," Federal Glass Co. 1931-1932. A scenic pattern of parrots sitting on bamboo branches.
   Colors: green, amber, some crystal and blue

Plate, 5" round, $995.

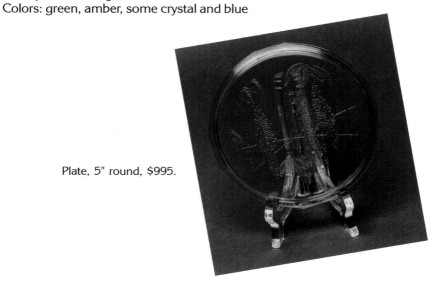

Petalware, MacBeth-Evans Glass Co. 1930-1940. This opaque, hand painted glassware has the motif of a beautifully decorated blue bird.
   Colors: monax, cremax, pink, crystal, cobalt and fired on red, blue, green and yellow.

(L-R) Plates, 8", $35-$40 each; Plate, 11", $50; Plates, 8", $35-$40.

2. Beaded

Beaded Block, Imperial Glass Co. 1927 - late 1930s. A popular pattern of vertical beaded lines, rows of beaded squares with a beaded top and bottom.

Colors: ice blue, pink, green, crystal, canary, iridescent, amber, red, opalescent, and milk white.

Vase, 6", $45.

Sugar, $17.

Beaded Edge, Pattern #22 Milk Glass, Westmoreland Glass Co. Late 1930s-1950s. An attractive pattern in white with the distinctive beaded edge, featuring hand painted decorations of fruits, flowers, and birds.

Plate, 10-1/2" dinner, $45.

Plate, 7" salad, $15 each.

Candlewick, Imperial Glass Co. 1936-1984. Elegant crystal glassware with outstanding or unique beaded edges.

Colors: crystal, blue, pink, yellow, black, red, cobalt blue, and a few items in color recently.

Bowl, 5" single handled, heart shaped, $22; Salt and Pepper Shakers, $15 pair; Bowl, 6" round divided two handled, $25.

Candleholders, 3-1/2" with finger hold, large beaded, $60 pair.

Ashtrays, crystal, $9; amber, $11.

Sugar, domed footed, $135; Creamer, domed footed, $135.

13

Columbia, Federal Glass Co. 1938-1942. Pattern has a bull's eye design in the center surrounded by a sunburst with large beading inside the rim. Outer rim is decorated with radial rows of graduated beads.

Colors: crystal and some pink (rare).

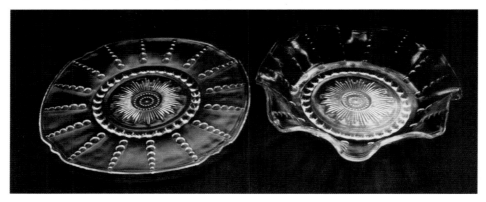

Plate, 11" chop, $17; Bowl, 10-1/2" ruffled edge, $22.

Dewdrop, Jeannette Glass Co. 1936-1956. Pattern has panels of fine beading and ribbed lines.

Colors: crystal and iridized.

Tray, 13" Lazy Susan, complete two piece set with ball
bearing ring, $45.

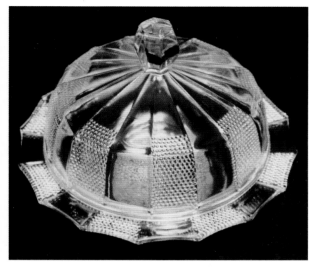

Butter Dish and Cover, $28.

Harp, Jeannette Glass Co. 1954-1957. A beautiful pattern with a musical name featuring a harp or lyre, with a dainty allover beading even on the bottom.

Colors: crystal, crystal with gold trim, iridescent, white, red, ice blue, and shell pink.

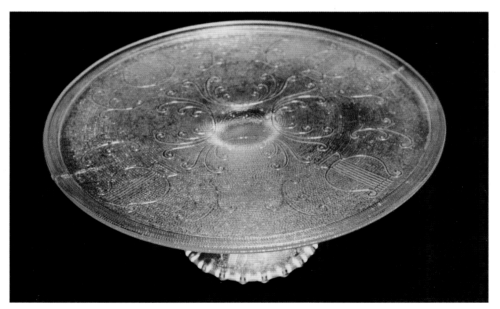

Cake Stand, 9", $25.

Ashtray, $5; Coasters, $4.

Heritage, Federal Glass Co. 1940-1955. A striking pattern in crystal with a flower design in a petal and an extensive beaded effect.

Colors: crystal, some pink, blue, green, and cobalt blue.

Plate, 12" sandwich, $15.

Bowl, 10-1/2" fruit, $16.

Bowl, 5" berry, $8; Bowl, 8-1/2" large berry, $40; Bowl 5" berry, $8.

Oyster and Pearl, Hocking Glass Co. 1938-1940. A very appealing design, the rim has double ribs with pearl-like beads in between and a scalloped edge.
Colors: pink, crystal, royal ruby, vitrock with fired on pink, blue and green.

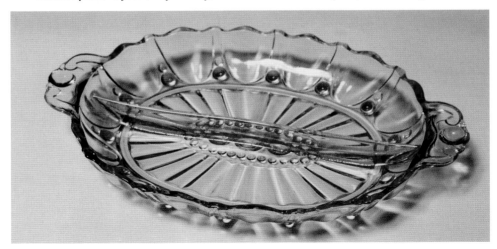

Relish dish, 10-1/2" oblong, divided, $18 in pink.

Candleholders, pair in royal ruby, $65; in pink, $40; in crystal, $40.

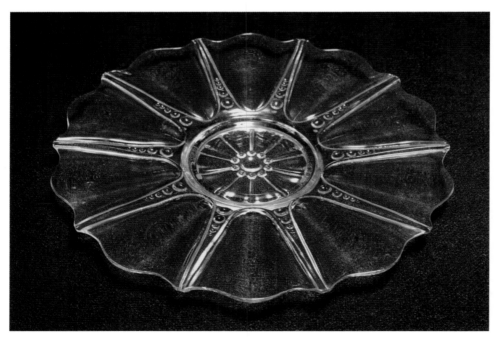

Plate, 13-1/2" sandwich, $20 in crystal.

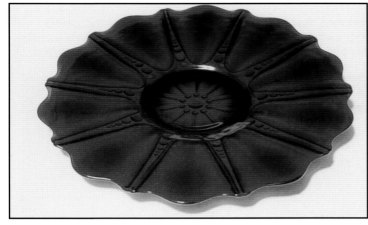

Plate, 13-1/2" sandwich, $55 in royal ruby.

Plate, 13-1/2" sandwich, $20 in pink.

Teardrop, #301, Duncan & Miller Glass Co. 1936-1955. An elegant crystal pattern featuring a finely beaded ring in the center and large beads tapering to smaller beads on the edge.

Colors: crystal.

Nut Dish, 6" two part, $11.

Roulette, "Many Windows," Hocking Glass Co. 1935-1938. Pattern has a center outburst of radial lines and a border of block shapes in the center of the rim. Characterized by indentations in rows similar to the appearance on a roulette wheel with a sunburst.

Colors: green, pink, and crystal.

Sherbet, $6; Plate, 8-1/2" luncheon, $8.

Yorktown, Federal Glass Co. Mid 1950s. Pattern consists of rows of rectangular blocks.

Colors: yellow, crystal, white, iridized, and smoke.

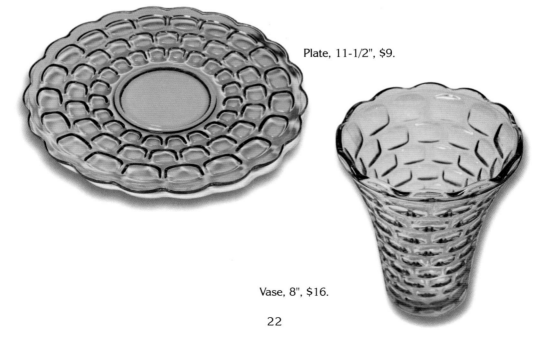

Plate, 11-1/2", $9.

Vase, 8", $16.

4. Bubbles

Bubble, Provincial Anchor Hocking Glass Co. 1940-1965. This pattern has its own category, since it is so easy to recognize (especially for novice collectors). It also remains one of the more popular patterns. It has scalloped edges and centers with a radial sunburst ending in a circle of bull's eye dots.

Colors: crystal, blue, pink, yellow, red, cobalt blue, plus a few items in color recently.

Sugar, $12; Creamer, $12 in green.

Bowl, 4" berry, $15 in iridescent.

Sugar, $25;
Creamer, $35 in
blue (rare).

Plate, 9-3/8"grill,
$23 in blue (rare).

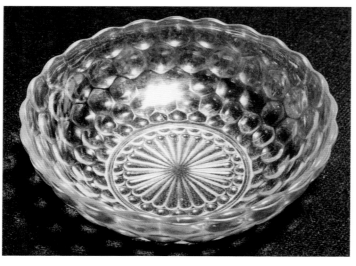

Bowl, 4" berry, $19 in
blue.

Candlestick, pair, $22 in crystal.

(L-R) Bowl, 5-1/4" cereal, $15; Bowl, 4-1/2" fruit, $15; Bowl, 4-1/2", $15.

Bowl, 8-3/8" berry, $20 in royal ruby.

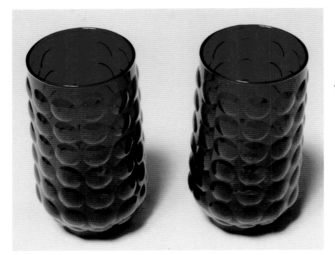

Tumblers, 9 oz. water, $9 in red.

Stemware, "Boopie" juice, $10; water, $12; juice, $10.

Bowl, 8-3/8" berry, $12 in pink.

Plate, 9-3/8" dinner, $7 in crystal.

5. Circles or Rings

Circle, Hocking Glass Co. 1930s. Pattern is easily recognized by the bands of circles throughout the pieces of glassware.
Colors: green, pink, and crystal.

Tumbler, 3-1/2" 4 oz. juice, $4 each.

Sherbet, 3-1/8", $5 in green.

Moderntone, Hazel Atlas Glass Co. 1934-1946. Late 1940s-1950s. This is an admired pattern for its rich coloring and for its simplistic style with widely spaced concentric rings that typify the art style of the 1930s.

Colors: amethyst, cobalt blue, crystal, pink, and platonite fired on colors.

Sherbet, $15;
Creamer, $12;
Sherbet, $15;
Plate, 8-7/8"
dinner, $18.

Cream Soup, $22;
Plate, $13; Cup, $11;
Saucer, $3.

Sugar, $5;
Creamer,
$5 in
crystal.

Moderntone Platonite, Hazel Atlas Glass Co. 1940s - early 1950s. This pattern has a simplistic style with widely spaced concentric rings in fired on colors—the look of the 30s.

Colors: platonite pastel, white, white decorated, dark fired on platonite.

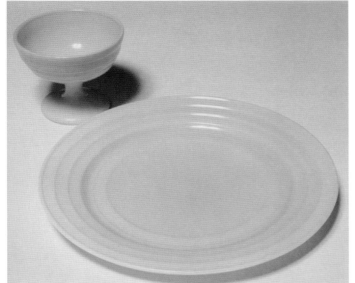

Sherbet, $5; Plate, 8-7/8" dinner, $6.

Cup, $4; Saucer, $1.

Plate, 8-7/8" dinner, $6: Cup, $4: Salt and Pepper Shakers, $16.

Old English, "Threading," Indiana Glass Co. Late 1920s. This pattern has very fine tightly threaded bands throughout the pieces of glassware.

Colors: green, amber, pink, crystal, crystal with flashed colors, and forest green.

Sherbet, $20.

Ovide, Hazel Atlas Glass Co. 1930-1935. This pattern has many variations of colors and designs. The popular yellow has a distinct black band or circle around the edge of the pieces. This particular set, yellow and then the black ring surrounding the pieces, is an attractive luncheon set.

Colors: green, black, white platonite trimmed with fired on colors in the 1950s.

Bowl, 5-1/2" cereal, $13; Plate, 9" dinner, $12; Cup and Saucer, $9.

Ring, "Banded Rings," Line #300, Hocking Glass Co. 1927-1932. A popular pattern of crystal decorated with the various colors in horizontal ribbed bands molded in a circle design. Called "circle design" with the horizontal ribbed bands. An early pattern in Depression Glass, but looks modern today.

Colors: crystal, crystal (with bands of pink, red, blue, orange, yellow, black, silver etc.) green, pink, "mayfair" blue, and royal ruby.

Creamer, in crystal, $6; Vase, 8", $35; Sugar, $6.

Cocktail Shakers, $30 each.

Pitcher, 8-1/2", 80 oz., $35.

31

Sugar, $5; Creamer, $5 in crystal.

Tally Ho, Line #1402, Cambridge Glass Co. 1932-1940s. This pattern has fine narrow, horizontal circles from the bottom, half way up on the pieces.
Colors: crystal, amber, carmen, forest green, and royal ruby

Cocktail, $3 each in crystal.

6. Cubes

American, Fostoria Glass Co. 1915-1986. An elegant pattern that consists of brilliant crystal cubes throughout the glassware.

Colors: Crystal, some amber, blue, green, yellow (late 20s), pink tinting to purple, white, and currently in red and crystal.

Bowl, 11" centerpiece tri-corner, $45.

Bowl, 4-1/2" round, one handled, $10; Bowl, 4-1/2" heart shaped (tri-corner) one handled, $12.

Plate, 7" salad, $10; Tumbler, $15; Plate, 7" salad, $10.

Hat, $65.

American, "Whitehall," (1986 or earlier), Fostoria Glass Co. 1915-1986; Indiana Glass Co. 1987-?. Originally made by Fostoria until Lancaster Colony bought the company. Before the actual purchase of Fostoria, Lancaster Colony marketed a similar pattern called "Whitehall" that was produced by Indiana Glass.

Colors: crystal, some amber, green, blue, yellow, pink tinting to purple (late 1920s), white and red (1980s)

Punch Bowl, with cranberry ring decorated, $200-$225. Entire set with cups, $425-$450. Cups, $22 each; set of twelve, $264.

Cube, "Cubist," Jeannette Glass Co. 1929-1933. A pattern in both name and shape, consisting of diamond cut crystal deeply indented cubes. An "eye-catching" design.

Colors: green, pink, crystal, amber, white, ultramarine, canary yellow, and blue

Plate, 8" luncheon in green, $9; Sherbet, footed, $9; Cup, $9; Saucer, $3.

Plate, 8" luncheon in pink, $9; Creamer, 2-5/8", $3; Sugar, 2-3/8", $3.

Tray, 7-1/2" (for sugar and creamer), $4; Creamer, 3-9/16", $2; Sugar, 3-9/16", $2 in crystal.

Hex Optic, "Honey Comb," Jeannette Glass Co. 1928-1932. Pattern has hexagonal shaped "optic" depressions in a circular cubic or block formation.
Colors: pink, green, ultra marine (late 1930s), and iridescent (1950s)

Cup, $7; Saucer, $3; Plate, 8" luncheon, $6 in green.

7. Diamonds

Diamond Point, Indiana Glass Co. Late 1950s-1980s. This pattern has a distinct pointed four sided diamond design throughout the glassware except for a clear band at the top, with variations in molds and colors.

Colors: crystal, crystal with ruby stain, crystal with gold, blue satin, green satin, black, yellow, teal, blue, amber, electric blue, carnival, and milk

Plate, 14-1/2" serving, $15 in crystal with ruby trim.

Compote, covered candy, $15 in crystal with ruby trim.

Compote, covered candy, $20 in electric blue.

Compote, covered candy, saw-tooth, mitre diamond, $20 in black.

Diamond Quilted, "Flat Diamond," Imperial Glass Co. Late 1920s to early 1930s. A simple pressed pattern with a quilted diamond effect.

Colors: pink, blue, green, crystal, black, some red, and amber

Candleholders, $14 each; Bowl, 7", $16.

Creamer, $12; Sugar, $12.

English Hobnail, Line #555, Westmoreland Glass Co. 1917-1940s and a few through 1980s. The hobs on this pattern are more rounded and feel smooth to the touch.

Colors: pink, crystal, turquoise ice blue, blue, cobalt blue, green, lilac, red and red flashed, amber, opalescent, black, and milk

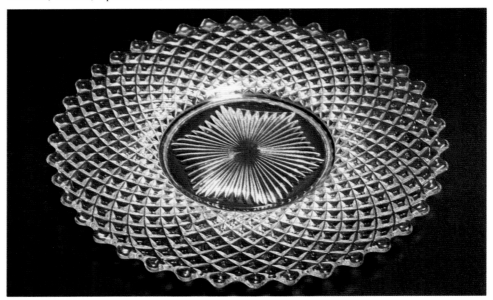

Plate, 10" round, $45.

Little Jewel, "Diamond," Line #330, Imperial Glass Co. Early 1930s. An attractive pattern, which is becoming more popular today, consisting of rows of diamond blocks with a sunburst bottom and a beaded edge.

Colors: black, crystal, green, iridescent, pink, white, and yellow

Vase, bouquet, $18; Celery Tray, 8-1/2", $23.

Miss America, Hocking Glass Co. 1935-1938. This pattern enjoys great popularity with its distinctive, easy-to-recognize sunburst of radial lines, hobnail and points. Colors: crystal, pink, some green, ice blue, jadeite, and royal ruby

Platter, 12-1/4" oval, $15 in crystal.

Compote, 5", $18.

Cup and Saucer, $12.

Relish, 8-3/4" four part, $25.

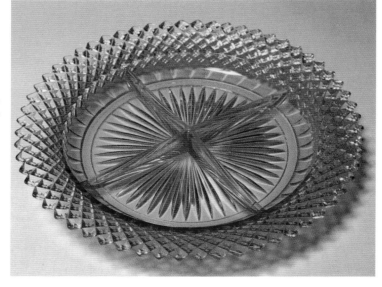

Bowl, 8" curved in at top, $95.

Shell Pink Milk Glass, Jeannette Glass Co. 1957-1959. This pattern was produced in numerous designs with "diamond beaded" being just one of the patterns.
Colors: opaque pink

Compote, 6" Windsor, $22.

Waterford, "Waffle," Hocking Glass Co. 1933-1944. The distinctive rim of Waterford has a lattice or waffle design with a triple concentric circle of small blocks.
Colors: crystal, pink, some yellow, vitrock, and forest green (1950s)

Bowl, 8-1/4" large berry, $28.

Tumbler, 4-7/8", 10 oz. footed, $15; Plate, 6" sherbet, $4.

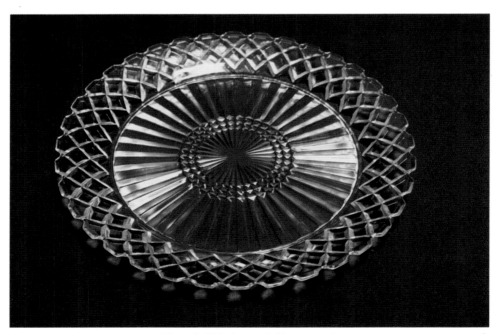

Plate, 9-5/8" dinner, $12 in crystal.

Windsor, "Windsor Diamond," Jeannette Glass Co. 1936-1946. A pressed pattern resembling cut crystal that consists of a series of diamond shaped facets emanating from a circle of radial ribs.

Colors: pink, green, crystal, some delphite, amberina red, and ice blue

Sugar, with cover, $12 in crystal; Creamer, $5.

Bowl, 7" x 11-3/4" boat shaped, $40.

Bowl, 9" two handled, $22.

Bowl, 7-1/8" three legs, $9.

Platter, 11-1/2" relish, $15.

8. Fancy Rim

Canterbury, #115, Duncan & Miller Glass Co. 1937. An elegant pattern with a flared or scalloped rim and some large vertical panels.

Colors: crystal, sapphire blue, cape cod, blue, chartreuse, ruby, cranberry, pink, jasmine, and yellow

Vase, 8-1/2" x 6", $70 in blue.

Christmas Candy, #624, Indiana Glass Co. 1937-early 1950s. This pattern has a rim of continuous loops, which resemble the old-fashioned ribbon Christmas candy.

Colors: terrace green (teal) and crystal

Plate, 11-1/4" sandwich, $15.

Crocheted Crystal, Imperial Glass Co. 1943 - early 1950s. Crystal in an elegant pattern with an open lace rim also featuring large lines radiating from the center.
Colors: crystal

Bowl, 10-1/2" salad, $30.

Candleholder, $15; Plate, 9-1/2", $13; Candleholder, $15.

Lariat, Blank #1540, A.H. Heisy & Co. An elegant pattern in fine crystal with a very fine unique loop edging.

Colors: crystal, black (rare), and amber (rare)

Plate, 8" salad, $22.

Mt. Pleasant, "Double Shield," L. E. Smith Glass Co. 1920s-1934. This pattern in black has scalloped edges with alternating one and two points making it easy to identify.

Colors: black amethyst, amethyst, cobalt blue, crystal, pink, green, and white

Candleholders, pair, $30.

Bowl, 6" two handled, $18.

Plate, 6" two handled, $16.

Sherbet, $6; Saucer, $7.

Newport, "Hairpin," Hazel Atlas Glass Co. 1936-1940. An attractive pattern called "Hairpin" by some collectors. It has overlapping hairpin lines on the borders.

Colors: cobalt blue, amethyst, some pink, platonite white, and fired on colors.

Plate, 8-13/16" dinner, $30 in amethyst.

Old Colony, "Laced Edge," Hocking Glass Co. 1935-1938. A pressed pattern with a center consisting of a sunburst design (radiating lines or ridges) and a pierced or open border design.

Colors: pink, some crystal, and green

Plate, 10-1/2" relish, three part, $30.

Bowl, 9-1/2" plain, $32.

Plate, 7-1/4" salad, $30.

Flower Bowl, with crystal frog, $30.

Radiance, New Martinsville Glass Co. 1936-1939. This is a fine elegant glassware in the Depression Glass line with a variety of unique items.
Colors: red, cobalt blue, ice blue, amber, crystal, pink, and emerald green

Creamer, $15; Sugar, $15 in amber.

Silver Crest, Fenton Art Glass Co. 1943-present. A very attractive white glass (milk glass) with edging encompassing crystal ruffled and crimped edges.

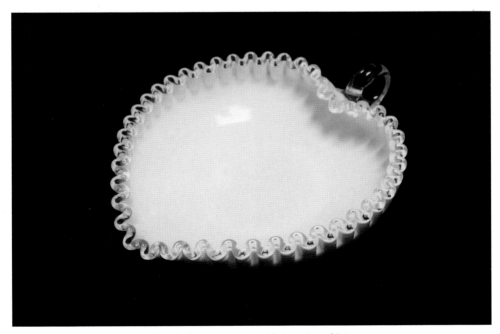

Relish, heart shaped with handles, $24.

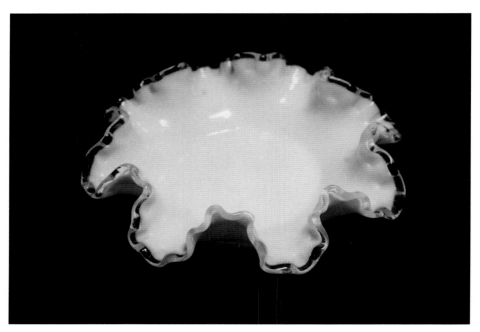

Bowl, 8-1/2", $30.

Tidbit, crimped two tiered plate, luncheon or dessert, $50.

9. Figures

Chinex Classic, MacBeth-Evans Division of Corning Glass Works. Late 1930s-early 1940s. A popular pattern with different decorated designs. The Windsor Castle decal is among the most popular.
Colors: Ivory, Ivory with decal decoration

Bowl, 9" vegetable, $40; Plate, 6-1/4" sherbet, $8; Plate, 9-3/4" dinner, $20.

Coin Glass, Line #1372, Fostoria Glass 1958-1982. An easy pattern to identify due to the coin design in the glassware and the scalloped edge.
Colors: amber, blue, crystal, green, olive, and red

Bowl, 5-3/8" handled, $20.

Early American Prescut, Anchor Hocking Glass Corp. 1960-1999. Pattern with a star design and a sunburst ray cut deeply into its center.
Colors: amber, crystal, blue, green, red, and black

Sugar, with lid, $5 in amber.

Sugar, with lid, $4; Creamer, $3; Bowl, 6-3/4" footed, $5.

King's Crown, "Thumbprint," Line #4016, U.S. Glass Co, Tiffin, late 1800s-1960. Indiana Glass Co. 1970s. Pieces made by Tiffin have elongated thumbprint patterns with a star design in the center, while Indiana pieces are plain and have circular thumbprints.

Colors: crystal, crystal and ruby or cranberry flash, crystal with gold or platinum

Plate, 14" relish, five part, $125 in ruby flash.

Compote with cover, $10 in crystal.

Moon and Star, L. G. Wright. 1930s-1960s; L. E. Smith. 1940s. This pattern has the distinct moon and star design including an upper row with center stars.

Colors: crystal, amber, amberina, amethyst, blue, blue satin, opalescent, brown, cranberry, green, green satin, mint and opalescent milk glass, various ruby colors, vaseline, and jadeite

Toothpick, 3", $10 in green;
Compote, 6-1/2", $15;
Toothpick, 3", $10 in amber.

Ships, "Sailboat," "Sportsman Series," Hazel Atlas Co. Late 1930s. Although this pattern is scarce, it remains very popular, especially in cobalt blue with the white ship design in mint condition.

Colors: cobalt blue with white, yellow, red decoration, and crystal with blue

(Back, L-R) Ice Bowl, $40; Pitcher with lip, $75; Pitcher without lip, $65; Plate, $30 (Front, L to R) Tumbler, water, $11; Tumbler, roly poly, $12; Bowl, $35; Tumbler, juice, $14; Tumbler, heavy bottom, $28; Tumbler, heavy bottom, $28.

Snowflake (company unknown). 1920s-1930s. A type of cake plate with a large snowflake design, very distinctive, with a groove around the rim for insertion of the lid.

Colors: green and pink

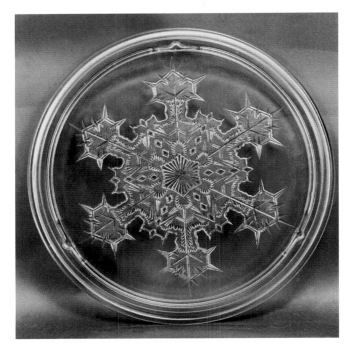

Cake Plate, 12-3/4", $35-$40.

Star, Federal Glass Co. Late 1950s-early 1960s. This pattern has a striking star with an outburst of rays.
Colors: yellow, crystal, and crystal with gold trim

Plate, 11" round, $12.

Pitcher, 7" 60 oz., $12.

Stars and Stripe, Anchor Hocking Glass Co. 1942. This pattern resembles Queen Mary but differs with the inner circle of stars and a patriotic symbol of an eagle emblem in the center of the plate.
Colors: crystal

Plate, 8", $18.

10. Filigree

American Sweetheart, MacBeth-Evans Glass Co. 1931-1936. A delicate pattern with a neat arrangement consisting of a center motif of festoons, ribbons, and scroll, with smaller ones surrounding the scalloped rim and including short radial lines to the border.

Colors: pink, monax, ruby, cobalt, some cremax, and some color trimmed monax

Platter, 12", $30 in pink.

Baroque, Line #2496, Fostoria 1936-1966. A soft yellow color called topaz in an elegant glassware line, which consists of a petal like handle, footed bottom, and a flower like design on some pieces.

Colors: crystal, azure blue, topaz, red, blue, and black amethyst

Bowl, 4" handled, footed, $20; Bowl, 6-1/2" two part, $20.

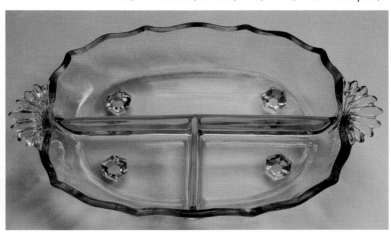

Bowl, 10" relish, three part, $30.

Bowknot, Belmont Tumbler Co. Late 1920s. Design is characterized by a unique bow with ribbons and a floral motif in a scroll type design.

Colors: green

Tumbler, 5" 10 oz. footed, $25.

Cameo, "Ballerina," "Dancing Girl," Hocking Glass Co. 1930-1934. This is the only pattern in Depression Glass that has a human figure. It features little dancing girls with long draped scarves appearing in the borders of the plates surrounded by festoons and ribbon bows.

Colors: green, yellow, pink, and crystal with platinum rim

Cup, $9; Saucer, $3; Tumbler, 4" 9 oz., $30.

Sugar, $20; Creamer, $22.

Plate, 9-1/2" dinner, $12.

Capri, Hazel Ware Division of Continental Can. 1960s. A filigree type pattern whose branches form a cluster of rotating leaves with a scroll sunburst in the center and a large sunburst on the bottom.

Colors: azure blue

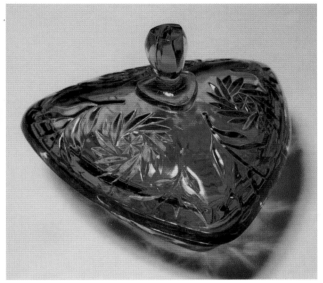

Candy jar with cover, footed triangular, $32.

Fire King Oven Glass, Anchor Hocking Glass Co. 1940s-1950s. A popular Depression Glass kitchen pattern with a sizable variety of versatile items featuring circles, dots, and bands. A definite filigree type.

Colors: sapphire blue, crystal, some ivory, and jadeite

Pie Plate, 9", $10

Madrid, Federal Glass Co. 1932-1939. Indiana Glass Co. 1980s. A scroll like design with some dots and an unusual filigree design.

Colors: green, pink, amber, crystal, and madonna blue

Sherbet, $7 in amber.

Sherbet, $12 in green.

Sherbet, $5 in crystal.

Bowl, 7" soup, $16.

Patrician, "Spoke," Federal Glass Co. 1933-1937. Plates have an irregular edge with a scalloped inner border and a center motif that is round with an eight spoke design surrounded by a scrolled ten pointed star.

Colors: pink, green, amber, and crystal

Plate, 10-1/2" dinner, $10.

Bowl, 8-1/2" large berry, $45.

Princess, Hocking Glass Co. 1931-1935. Plates are octagonal with a center motif of a snowflake with eight spokes. Rim pattern consists of lines, flowers and leaves. Colors: green, topaz, yellow, apricot yellow, pink, and light blue

Plate, 9-1/2" grill, $20 in pink.

Plate, 9-1/2" grill, $20 in green.

Bowl, 9-1/2" hat shaped, $50.

Roxana, Hazel Atlas Glass Co. 1932. This pattern has a unique four pointed design emanating in the form of a cross. The same motif with three leaf like design adorns the border along alternating sides.

Colors: golden topaz, crystal, and some white

Bowl, 6" cereal, $20: Sherbet, $12.

Royal Lace, Hazel Atlas Glass Co. 1934-1941. An outstanding, very decorative and elaborate pattern with a motif of lacy scrolls, leaves and flowers surrounded by a drape design.

Colors: cobalt blue, crystal, green, pink, and some amethyst

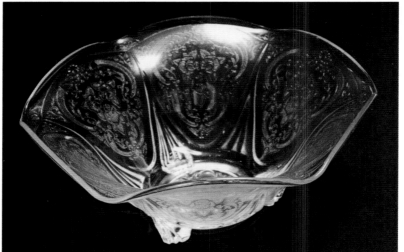

Bowl, 10" three legged, scalloped edge, $55.

Plate, 9-7/8" dinner, $18 in crystal.

Sugar, $40 in blue.

11. Floral

Adam, Jeannette Glass Co. 1932-1934. A beautiful pattern with the center consisting of a group of alternating feathers, plumes, and wide radial ridges and rims.
Colors: pink, green, and crystal

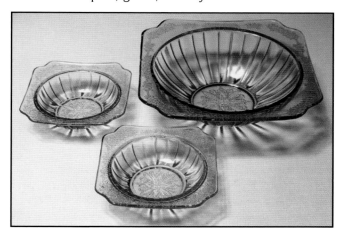

(L-R) Bowl, 4-3/4" berry or dessert, $25; Bowl, 9", $45; Bowl, dessert, $25.

Cake Plate, 10" footed, $30.

Camellia, Jeannette Glass Co. 1950s. An attractive pattern in crystal with a camellia (flower) design in the bottom of some pieces or in the center.
Colors: crystal, crystal with gold trim, iridized, flashed red, and blue

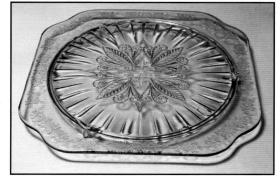

Bowl, 10-1/8" x 3-1/2" deep, $15 with gold trim; Candleholders, pair, $20.

Cherokee Rose, Tiffin Glass Co. 1940s-1950s. This is a pattern with a delicate etched rose design on the bottom with swirled lines emanating from the base.
Colors: crystal

Candlesticks, double branched, pair, $110.

Cloverleaf, Hazel Atlas Glass Co. 1930-1936. Center pattern of the plate has a six pointed star surrounded by clover motifs pointing toward the center of the plate. The border has curved stems of clover in a scalloped pattern.
Colors: pink, green, yellow, crystal, and black

Cup, $9; Saucer, $3.

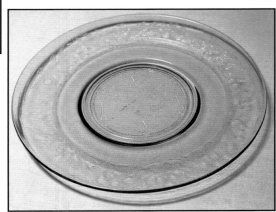

Plate, 8" luncheon, $8.

Cremax, MacBeth-Evans Division of Corning Glass Works. Late 1930s-1940s. This pattern in cremax, with the piecrust edging, has colored bands on the border of the pieces, fired on band trims, and decal decorations; the floral is a very popular design.

Colors: cremax, cremax with fired on colored trim or decals

Plate, 11-1/2" sandwich, $20.

Bowl, 5-3/4" cereal, $10;
Plate, 9-3/4" dinner, $12;
Cup, $5; Saucer, $3.

Daisy, #620, Indiana Glass Co. 1930s. A pattern with the design of daisies found around the border, giving it its characteristic motif.

Colors: crystal (1933-1940), fired on red (late 1930s), amber (1940s), dark green, and milk glass (1960s, 1970s, 1980s)

Relish Dish, 8-3/8" three part, $25.

Tumblers, 9 oz. footed, $22 each.

Bowl, 7-3/8" deep berry, $9; Plate, 9-3/8" dinner, $7.

Creamer, footed, $6; Sugar, footed, $9.

Dogwood, "Apple Blossom," "Wild Rose," MacBeth-Evans Glass Co. 1929-1932. An overall floral pattern. The plates have three large blossoms with foliage as a center motif, while the surrounding rim is decorated with dogwood blossoms and leaves.
Colors: pink, green, some crystal, monax, cremax, and yellow

Plate, 8" luncheon, $7.

Fire King – "Fleurette," Hocking Glass Corp. 1958-1960. White with floral decal, attractive for dinnerware.
Colors: white with decal

Snack set includes: Plates, with a beaded edge; Tray, 11" x 6", $4; Cup, 5 oz., $3.

Fire King – "Peach Lustre," "Laurel," Anchor Hocking Glass Corp. 1952-1963. This pattern has a leaf design in a circle formation near the top of each piece of glassware.
Colors: peach

Sugar, footed, $4; Creamer, footed, $4.

74

Fire King – "Primrose," Anchor Hocking Glass Corp. 1960-1962. This pattern was produced for dinnerware and ovenware. The embossed floral primrose design adds to the solid white.

Colors: white with decal

Plate, 9-1/8" dinner, $7.

Fire King – "Wheat," Anchor Hocking Glass Corp. Late 1960s. An anchor white pattern, which remains very popular and most prolific with the wheat motif.

Colors: white with wheat

Platter, 9" x 12", $14.

Candy or Cheese Dish, 6-3/4" with cover, $55.

Floragold, "Louisa," Jeannette Glass Co. 1950s. A pattern of branches and leaves interlocking with flowers. An overall design.

Colors: iridescent, shell pink, and crystal

Pitcher, 64 oz., $40.

Sugar, $7; Candy Dish, one handle, $12; Creamer, $9.

Floral, "Poinsettia," Jeannette Glass Co. 1931-1935. A beautiful pattern in a floral poinsettia design with vertical panels.

Colors: pink, green, delphite, jadeite, crystal, amber, red, black, and custard yellow

Sugar, $12.

Floral and Diamond Band, U.S. Glass Co. Late 1920s. This pattern has a deeply cut floral and diamond design band.

Colors: pink, green, iridescent, black, and crystal

Sugar, $15; Sugar Lid, $65; Creamer, $20.

Pitcher, 8", $135; Tumbler, 4" water, $25; Tumbler, 5" iced tea, $50.

Florentine #1, "Poppy #1,"
Hazel Atlas Glass Co. 1932-1935.
This pattern has a six-sided style with
scalloped edges between the straight
edges. Center motif of flowers and
scrolls in a pinwheel shape is prominent. Borders have elaborate scroll-
ing with flowers resembling poppies.

Colors: pink, green, crystal, yellow, and cobalt blue

Plate, 8-1/2" salad, $8.

Florentine #2, "Poppy #2," Hazel
Atlas Glass Co. 1932-1935. A sister pattern to "Poppy #1." It has the same floral
motif except for the rims, which are plain
and round.

Colors: pink, green, yellow, crystal,
cobalt blue, amber, and ice blue

Pitcher, 7-1/2" 28 oz. footed, $35.

Indiana Custard, "Flower and Leaf Band," Indiana Glass Co. Early 1930s (white
1950s). The white is a neat pristine pattern made in the 1950s, whose pattern consists of a band of flowers and leaves along each edge.

Colors: Ivory or custard and white

Creamer, $17;
Sugar, $17

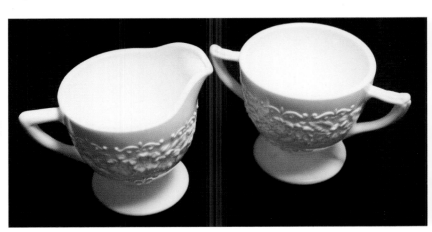

Iris, "Iris and Herringbone," Jeannette Glass Co. 1928-1932, 1950-1970. Very appealing with the unusual, large spray of iris with its blade-like leaves emanating from one point at the inner rim creating a bouquet effect.

Colors: crystal, iridescent, some pink, some green, bi-colored (red/yellow and blue/green combinations), and yellow

Pitcher, 9-1/2" footed, $42 in iridescent.

Pitcher, 9-1/2" footed, $40; Tumblers, 6" footed, $20 each.

Jubilee, Lancaster Glass Co. Early 1930s. Elaborately decorated with an exquisite floral engraving of an elegant flower and leaf design containing twelve petals with an open center.

Colors: yellow, crystal, and pink

Candlesticks, pair, $185.

Tray, 11" center handled, $210.

Sugar, $35; Creamer, $35 in pink.

Lorain, "Basket," #615, Indiana Glass Co. 1929-1932. An attractive pattern that contains conventional baskets of flowers, a center motif of scrolls, and garlands surrounded by an eight-sided swag ending in finials and scrolls.
Colors: green, yellow, and crystal

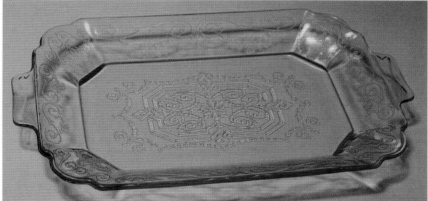

Platter, 11-1/2", $45.

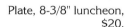

Plate, 8-3/8" luncheon, $20.

Lotus, Pattern #1921, Westmoreland Glass Co. 1921-1980. This pattern has a unique, deep petal edged trim with faint vertical lines.

Colors: amber, amethyst, black, blue, crystal, green, milk, pink, red and various applied trims and satinized colors.

Bowl, 9" cupped, $85.

Mayfair, "Open Rose," Hocking Glass Co. 1931-1937. This pattern consists of a center circle of roses with widely spaced lines, a border of roses, and is scalloped with square plates.

Colors: pink, green, blue, yellow, crystal, and satinized pink or blue

Cake Plate, 12" with handles, $55 in pink.

Bowl, 12" fruit, deep scalloped, $65.

Goblet, 9 oz, $80.

Normandie, "Bouquet and Lattice," Federal Glass Co. 1933-1940. This pattern has a motif of lattice and floral designs, round bouquet of flowers surrounded by a ribbon and flower wreaths.

Colors: iridescent, amber, and pink

Cup, $11 in pink.

Sugar, $9; Creamer, $9.

Plate, grill, $11 in iridescent.

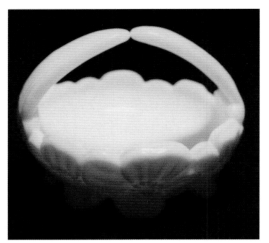

Pansy Basket, Line #757, Westmoreland Glass Co. 1970. White milk glass decorated with a variety of colors and the pansy pattern.

Colors: white, white decorated with various colors, antique blue, green and purple marble, crystal, mint, blue flame, and crystal with ruby stain and mist

Basket with split handle, decorated with pansies, $22.

Patrick (Jubilee's Brother Pattern), Lancaster Glass Co. Early 1930s. Pattern has a delicate design of a three flowered bouquet in the center surrounded by flowers on either side of connecting leaves and vines.

Colors: yellow and pink

Goblet, 6" 10 oz. water, $70; Creamer, $38; Plate, 8" luncheon, $25; Sugar, $38.

Petal, #2829, Federal Glass Co. Pattern characterized by various petal designs in a stylized manner, with a center sunburst.

Colors: iridescent, flashed colors, crystal

Bowl, 10", $12 iridized.

Plate, 9", $8 in crystal.

Plates, 6", $6 in flashed colors.

Petalware, MacBeth-Evans Glass Co. 1930-1945. This opaque, hand painted glassware was intended to resemble ceramics. It has a versatile but simple floral design and was a very popular pattern, especially with the red trim.

Colors: monax, cremax, pink, crystal, cobalt and fired on red, blue, green, and yellow

Plate, 8" salad (monax with decorated flowers), $10; Plate, 8" salad (monax with decorated fruit), $10.

Plates, 6" sherbet, $3.

Creamer, footed, $12; Cup, $11; Saucer, $3; Sugar, footed, $10.

Pineapple and Floral, #618, Indiana Glass Co. 1932-1937. A pressed pattern in the sandwich glass tradition. Center motif is a flower surrounded by a pineapple type pressed design with a floral border.

Colors: crystal, amber, and fired on red

Platter, 11" closed handle, $15.

Plate, 11-1/2" sandwich, $20.

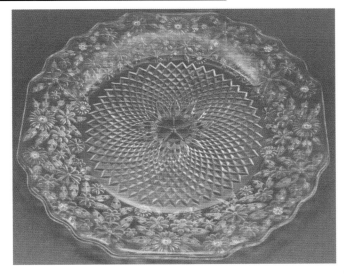

Rose Cameo, Belmont Tumbler Co. 1931. This pattern resembles the "Cameo" pattern except for the encircled rose in the decorated border. Rose Cameo was limited in production to seven pieces.

Colors: green

Tumbler, $25.

Rose Etching #1515, "Waverly Blank" #1519, A.H. Heisy and Co. 1949-1957. An elegant pattern of roses, with an edging of three beads and a point in between. Colors: crystal, amber (rare)

Plate, 7" salad, $20.

Rosemary, "Dutch Rose," Federal Glass Co. 1935-1937. Pattern has a center bouquet of roses with a rim of roses placed between an overlapping, looped design. Colors: amber, green, pink, and some iridized

Plate, dinner, $10.

Plates, 6-3/4" salad, $6 each.

Plate, grill, $30 in pink.

Rosepoint, Cambridge Glass Co. 1936-1953. An elegant pattern consisting of a pointed and profuse edge that surrounds the roses.
Colors: crystal and some crystal with gold trim

Relish, 8" three part - three handled, $40.

Sharon, "Cabbage Rose," Federal Glass Co. 1935-1939. A very popular and attractive pattern with a center motif of a curved spray of roses with spokes on the border.
Colors: pink, green, amber, and some crystal

Creamer, footed $20; Sugar, $14 in pink.

Bowl, 9-1/2" oval vegetable, $18 in amber.

Bowl, 5" berry, $14; Plate, 9-1/2" dinner, $22; Cup, $14.

Sunflower, Jeannette Glass Co. 1920s. Pattern has a stylized sunflower in the center surrounded on the border with large flowers and foliage.
Colors: pink, green, some delphite, some opaque colors, and ultramarine

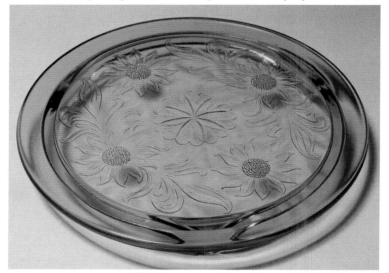

Cake Plate, $15.

Cake Plate, $15.

Creamer, $25; Sugar, $25 in pink.

Creamer, $25; Sugar, $25 in green.

Trivet, 7" three legged with turned up edges, $350.

Vitrock, Anchor Hocking Glass Co. 1934 (late 1930s) A beautiful set in white with floral trim.

Colors: white and white with fired on colors – usually red or green

Sugar, oval, $6; Creamer, oval, $6; Saucer, $3; Cup, $6; Bowl, 7-1/2" cereal, $8; Plate, 10" dinner, $10.

Wild Rose (with Leaves), Indiana Glass Co. 1940-1980s. Pattern has a distinct rose in the center surrounded by leaves with points and round hobs in between.

Colors: crystal, crystal satinized, iridescent, milk glass, multicolored (blue, green, pink, and yellow), satinized green, pink, and yellow (sprayed green, lavender, and pink)

Bowl, large vegetable, $10.

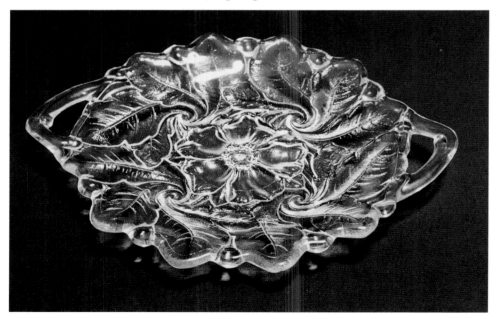

Tray, two handled, $15.

12. Fruits

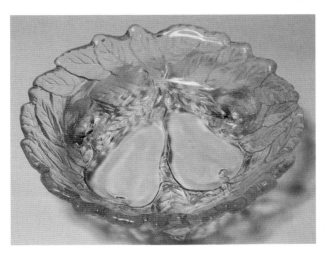

Avocado, "Sweet Pear," **#601** Indiana Glass Co. 1923-1933. Center of the bowl has a pear design in the bottom surrounded by a border of a leaf pattern.

Colors: pink, green, crystal, white (1950s); yellow mist, burnt honey, and water sets in myriad frosted and transparent colors for Tiara Home Products 1974-1998.

Bowl, 6" footed relish, $30.

Beaded Edge, Pattern #22 Milk Glass, Westmoreland Glass Co. Late 1930s-1950s. A milk glass pattern with decorations of fruit and floral.

Colors: white

Plate, 10-1/2" dinner, $45 in fruit cherry.

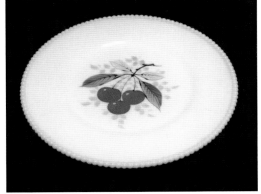

Plate, 10-1/2" dinner, $45; Plate, 7" salad, $15.

Cherry Blossom, Jeannette Glass Co. 1930-1939. A true Depression mold, consisting of an etched pattern in an opaque glass color with a profuse allover pattern.

Colors: pink, green, delphite (opaque blue), crystal, jadeite (opaque green), and red

Tray, 10-1/2" sandwich, $30.

Bowl, 9" two handled, $50.

Fruits, Hazel Atlas and other glass companies. 1931-1935. Pattern has numerous narrow panels with border sprays of cherries, grapes, pears, and a center of spray cherries.

Colors: pink, green, some crystal, and iridized

Cup, $8; Saucer, $6.

Paneled Grape, Pattern #1881, Westmoreland Glass Co. 1950-1970s. Milk glass decorated with a grape and vine design set within a panel base.
Colors: white, white with decorations, and some mint green (1970)

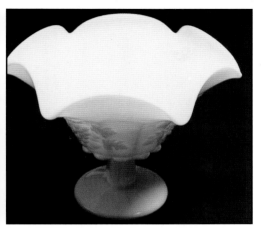

Compote, 4-1/2" footed ruffled, $30.

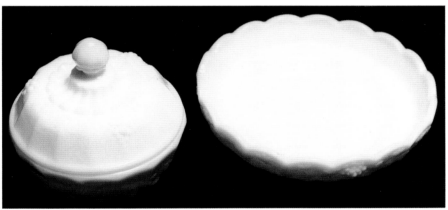

Puff box or Jelly with cover, $30; Bowl, 6-1/2", $23.

Petalware, MacBeth-Evans Glass Co. 1930-1940. This is opaque, hand painted glassware with ribbon trim and a fruit motif.
Colors: monax, cremax, pink, crystal, cobalt, fired on red, blue, green, and yellow

Plates, 8", $40-$50 each in lucretia dewberry, florence cherry, raspberry strawberry, and muscat.

Pineapple and Floral, #618, Indiana Glass Co. 1932-1937. A pressed pattern, with a center motif of a flower surrounded by a pineapple.

Colors: crystal, amber, some fired on red, green, milk, white (late 1960s), avocado, pink (1980s), and cobalt blue

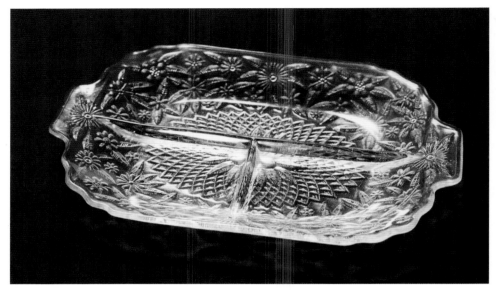

Platter/Relish Dish, 11-1/2" divided, $18.

Sugar, $9; Creamer, $9.

Pioneer, Line #2806, Federal Glass Co. 1940. This pattern features strong, heavy glass designed in a fruit motif with vertical panels that continue to the rim.

Colors: crystal, some pink and sprayed on colors

Bowl, 11" crimped, $15.

Plate, 12", $13; Bowl, 5-3/8" nappy, $8; Plate, 8", $8; Bowl, 5-3/8" nappy, $8.

Plantation, Blank #1567, A. H. Heisy & Co. A clear crystal pattern featuring a distinct pineapple design with a ruffled edge.

Colors: crystal, some pink and sprayed on

Marmalade with cover, $190.

Pretzel, Indiana Glass Co. Late 1930s-1980s. A pattern with an extreme design of crossed or x-shaped ribs and flared edges.

Colors: crystal, teal, avocado, and more recent issues in amber and blue

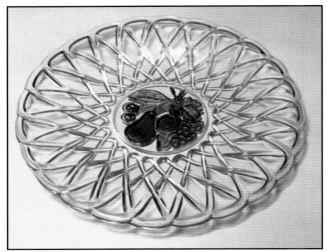

Plate, 9-3/8" dinner (embossed with fruit design in the middle), $12 painted.

Plate, 9-3/8" dinner (embossed with fruit design in the middle), $12 clear.

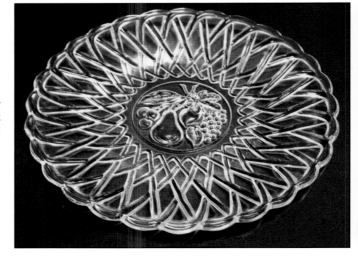

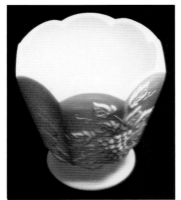

Shell Pink Milk Glass, Jeannette Glass Co. 1957-1959. A fashionable Jeannette pink milk color produced for a short time in the late 1950s. Has a delicate coloring that blends in beautifully with other pieces.

Colors: opaque pink

Bowl, "Napco" #2250, footed with berries, $15.

13. Geometric

"Big Top" Peanut Butter Glass, West Virginia Co. 1950s. An exquisite geometric style pattern in crystal.
Colors: crystal

Tumbler, 5-3/4" 10 oz., $8;
Sherbet, 3-5/8" 8 oz., $5.

Cape Cod, Imperial Glass Co. 1932-1980s An unusual design in elegant glassware with a sunburst in the center, a star design, and surrounded by a diamond like circle.
Colors: crystal, cobalt blue, and red

Salt and Pepper
Shakers, pair, $25;
Compote, $25.

Crackle, Imperial Glass Co. Mid 1920s. A very geometric style with an interesting network of "cracks" found throughout the pattern.

Colors: pink, green, amber, and crystal

Candlesticks, pair, $20.

Hex Optic, "Honey Comb," Jeannette Glass Co. 1928-1932. An early pressed pattern that has hexagonal shaped "optic" depressions.

Colors: pink, green, ultra marine (late 1930s), and iridescent (1950s)

Plate, 8" luncheon, $6.

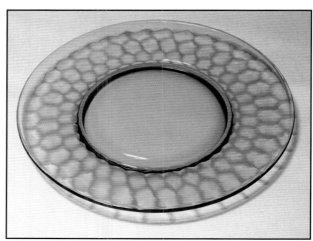

Mt. Vernon, "Washington," #699 (later), Imperial Glass Co. Late 1920s-1970s. A popular pattern in an overall formation, similar to a prismatic design.

Colors: crystal, red, green, yellow, milk, iridized, and red flash

Creamer, $12; Sugar, $12.

Pretzel, #622, Indiana Glass Co. Late 1930s-1980s. A pattern with an extreme design of interlocking loops or cross lines giving the appearance of diamonds in circles. Colors: crystal and teal

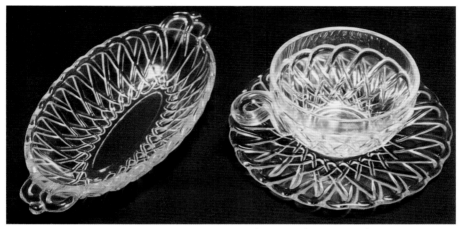

Pickle Dish, 8-1/2" two handled, $6; Cup, $6; Saucer, $1.

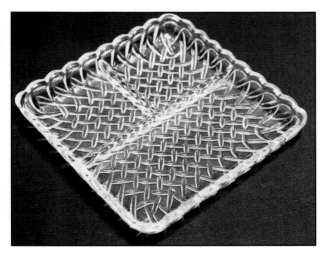

Plate, 7-1/4" square indent, three part, $9.

Sierra, "Pinwheel," Jeannette Glass Co. 1931-1933. The design of the pattern is a pinwheel shape, one of its kind, with the serrated edges. An art deco design.

Colors: green, pink, and some ultramarine

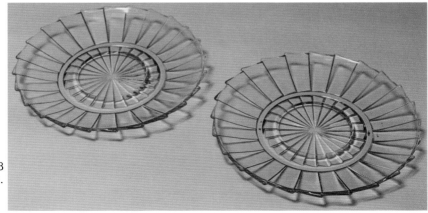

Saucers, $8 each.

Starlight, Hazel Atlas Glass Co. 1938-1940. This pattern has a center with a waffle design and borders that have cross over stippled lines, giving a plaid effect.
Colors: crystal, pink, some white, and cobalt

Creamer, oval, $8; Sugar, oval, $8.

Bowl, 5-1/2" cereal, closed handles, $7; Bowl, 5-1/2" cereal, closed handles, $7; Bowl, 8-1/2" closed handles, $10.

Tea Room, Indiana Glass Co. 1926-1931. A decorative art style of 20s and 30s, extreme in style, heavy pressed, and geometric with a flashy shape.
Colors: pink, green, amber, and some crystal

Sugar, footed, $20.

Thousand Lines, Anchor Hocking Glass Co. 1940-1960s. A pressed cut pattern of stars and bars and rainbow stars, which is also another name for this pattern. Uniquely designed.

Colors: crystal and satinized green

Tray, 12-1/2" sandwich, $13.

Bowl, 10-1/2" salad, flat base, $25.

14. Hobs & Dots

Capri, "Dots," Hazel Ware Division of Continental Can. 1960s. These pieces have numerous scattered dots on the glassware.

Colors: azure blue (main color), crystal, green, yellow, and amethyst in some designs

Tumbler, 6" 10 oz., $8 each.

Candy Jar with cover, $10.

Vase, $10.

Sugar, $20; Creamer, $12.

English Hobnail, Line #555, Westmoreland Glass Co. 1917-1940s, some 1980s. Centers of the pieces have rays of varying distances resembling a six point star effect. The abundance of hobs is more rounded, smoother to the touch in a diamond appearance.

Colors: pink, turquoise/ice blue, cobalt blue, green, lilac, red, opal trimmed blue, red flashed, black, blue, amber, and milk. Rare in red trim.

Plate, 10" round, $15.

Hobnail - Fenton Art Glass Co. Collectors are becoming more devoted to this wide variety of glassware.

Colors: white

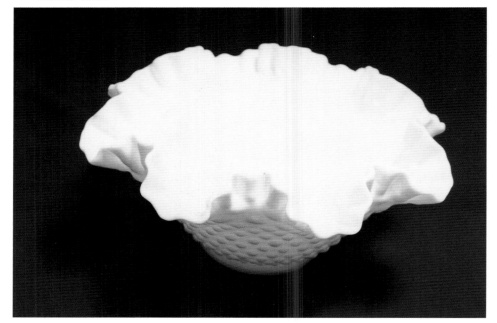

Bowl, 9" scalloped/flared, $60.

Vase, 5" doubled crimped, $18; Compote, 6" x 5-1/2" octagonal stemmed, $18.

Hobnail - Hocking Glass Co. 1934-1936. Pattern consists of circles of radiating raised hobs, which is a very popular and old pattern available in various colors. Colors: crystal, crystal with red trim, and pink

Cup, $6; Saucer/Sherbet plate, $4; Sherbet, $5 in pink.

Cup, $5; Saucer/Sherbet Plate, $4; Tumbler, 9 oz./10 oz. water, $6.

Decanter with stopper, $35; Tumblers, 3" – 3-1/2", $6 each.

Set of red trim crystal. (L-R) Sherbet, $6; Bowl, 5-1/2" cereal, $8; Plate, 8-1/2" luncheon, $8; Cup, $7; Saucer, $4.

(L-R) Tumbler, 9 oz, $9; Tumbler, 10 oz water, $10; Pitcher, $30; Whiskey, 1-1/2 oz., $9; Tumbler, 5 oz juice, $7; Tumbler 3 oz. footed wine, $10.

Moonstone, Hocking Glass Co. 1941-1946. A very attractive pattern in crystal with opalescent hobnails and rims giving a bluish effect.

Colors: crystal with opalescent hobnails, some green with opalescent hobnails, and other experimental colors.

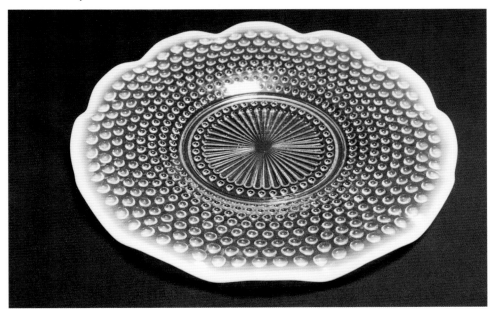

Plate, 10-3/4" sandwich, $28.

Heart bon bon, one handled, $15; Bowl, 5-1/2" crimped, dessert, $10; Bowl, 7-3/4", $12.

Opalescent, a very popular area of collecting. Adding bone ash chemicals to areas of an item while still hot and re-firing the object at tremendous heat attains the opalescent effect. Both pressed and mold-blown patterns are available to collectors.

Cake Plate, pedestal type, $100.

Tumblers, 3-3/4", $8-$10 each.

Creamer and Sugar set,
$25; Plate, $8.

Sugar and Creamer set,
$22.

Vase, cornucopia, $20.

Vase, bud, $20 in cobalt blue.

Salts, square, $10 each in green and blue.

Vase, scalloped and crimped, $20.

Bowl, crimped, $15; Candleholder, cornucopia style, $12.

Creamer and Sugar set, $20;
Mustard Dish with ladle, 2",
$18.

Raindrop, "Optic Design," Federal Glass Co. 1929-1933. A plain optic pattern with depressed "dots" or rounded bumps or hobs as the only decoration.
Colors: crystal and green

Cup and Saucer, $8.

15. Panel

Aurora, Hazel Atlas Glass Co. Late 1930s. A limited pattern featuring vertical panels with two bands around the top.

Colors: cobalt blue, pink, green, and crystal

Creamer, $25.

Bowl, 5-3/8" cereal, $19.

Colonial, "Knife and Fork," Hocking Glass Co. 1934-1936. A traditional style in the older glass with large panels tapered at the top with raised vertical lines in between. Entire glass has a paneled look.

Colors: pink, green, crystal, and vitrock

Sherbet, 3-3/8", $12.

Colonial Fluted, "Rope," Federal Glass Co. 1928-1933. A popular pattern in the older glass, which was used relentlessly showing much wear so is therefore limited to collect. It has distinct vertical panels with the edges fluted and roped.
Colors: green and crystal

Sugar, $10.

Fairfax, #2375, Fostoria Glass Co. 1927-1944. An elegant but plain pattern with large tapered panels.
Colors: blue, azure blue, orchid, amber, rose, green, topaz, some ruby, ebony, and wisteria

Compote, 7", $40.

Fortune, Hocking Glass Co. 1937-1938. A pattern with widely spaced radial ridges emanating from the center to a border of wider panels divided by straight radial lines.
Colors: pink and crystal

Bowl, 4-1/2" handled, $12; Bowl, 4-1/2" dessert, $12; Bowl, 4" berry, $10.

Newport, "Hairpin," Hazel Atlas Glass Co. 1936-1940. Most of the pieces have wide panels and some have overlapping hairpin lines on the borders.

Colors: cobalt blue, amethyst, some pink, platonite white, and fired on colors.

Sugar, $5; Creamer, $5.

Old Café, Hocking Glass Co. 1936-1940. Pattern has a center sunburst surrounded by a circle of widely spaced radiating lines. Rim has wide panels with two narrow lined panels.

Colors: pink, crystal, and royal ruby

Candy Dish, 8", $12 in crystal.

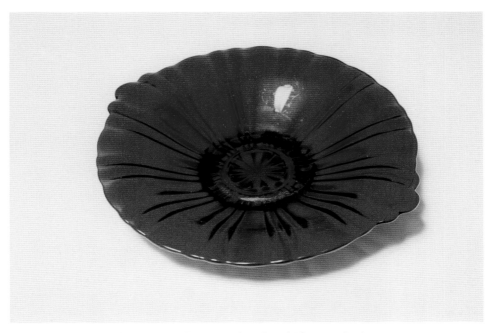

Candy Dish, 8" low tab handles, $18 in royal ruby.

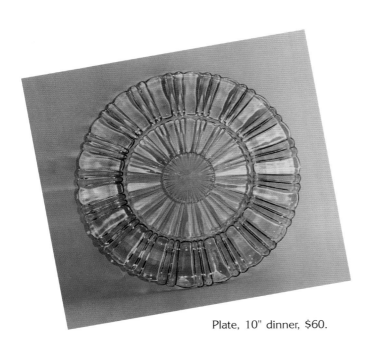

Plate, 10" dinner, $60.

Petalware, MacBeth-Evans Glass Co. 1930-1950. This pattern with the fluted panels and scalloped edges is a very versatile pattern and derives its name from the prominent petals.

Colors: monax, cremax, pink, crystal, cobalt blue, fired on blue, green, and yellow

Mustard Dish (with metal cover), $10 in cobalt blue only (without cover, $8).

Pillar Optic, **"Logs," "Log Cabin,"** Anchor Hocking Glass Co. 1937-1942. This pattern has panels that are evenly spaced with a plain or rounded top.

Colors: crystal, green, pink, royal ruby, amber, iridescent, and some cobalt

Tumblers, 9-12 oz., $15 each in cobalt blue (pink, $10 each).

Ribbon, Hazel Atlas Glass Co. Early 1930s. This pattern is distinguished by an arrangement of some evenly spaced small panels on certain pieces like bowls, while some panels on larger pieces expand in size at the top giving a flared look.

Colors: green and black

Candy Dish with cover, $45.

Round Robin, "Accordion Pleat" (possibly the Economic Glass Co.). 1927-1932. Vertical lines of fine panels ending in a plain ridge characterize this pattern.

Colors: green, iridescent, and some crystal

Sherbet, $10; Saucer, $2.

16. Ribbed

Anniversary, Jeannette Glass Co. 1947-1949, late 1960s, mid 1970s. This pattern consists of numerous vertical ribs with open clear spaces at the top of many pieces. Colors: pink, crystal, iridescent, and shell pink

Plate, 12-1/2" sandwich server, $10.

Tidbit, berry and fruit bowls with metal handles, $13.

Coronation, "Banded Rib," "Saxon," Hocking Glass Co. 1936-1940. The pieces in this pattern have a plain outer band with a border of inner circles of ridges and widely spaced lines in a band formation.

Colors: pink, green, crystal, and royal ruby

Bowl, 4-1/4" berry, handled, $7; Sherbet, $10; Bowl, 4-1/4" berry, $7.

Bowl, 4-1/4" berry, handled, $7; Bowl, 6-1/2" nappy, $6.

Bowl, 8" large berry handled, $15.

Crystolite, Blank #1503, A. H. Heisy and Co. An attractive pattern with a large ribbed design and a beaded trim.

Colors: crystal, zircon/limelight, sahara, and amber (rare)

Tray, 12" three part, $35.

Cheese, 5-1/2" footed, $27.

Manhattan, "Horizontal Ribbed," Anchor Hocking Glass Co. 1938-1943. This pattern is easily recognized with its horizontal, wide, sharp ribbed style.
Colors: crystal, pink, some green, ruby, and iridized

Bowl, 8" closed handles, $25; Bowl, 9-1/2" fruit, open handle, $35.

Candleholder, 4-1/2" square, $11; Bowl, 8" closed handle, $25.

Relish Tray, 14" with inserts, $85 in pink.

Relish Tray, 14" with inserts, $90 in royal ruby.

Candy Dish, 6-1/4" three legged, $15; Compote, 5-3/4", $40; Bowl, 5-3/8" berry, with handles, $24.

Pitcher, 80 oz tilted, $75.

National, Jeannette Glass Co. Late 1940s, mid 1950s. A heavy bold pattern with vertical ribs, dots at the base, and log like handles in cups, creamers, and sugar.
Colors: blue, crystal, pink, and shell pink

Tray, 8", $5; Sugar, $5; Creamer, $5.

New Century, Hazel Atlas Glass Co. 1930-1935. This pattern contains a small bull's eye center with widely spaced vertical lines leading to the border in a sunburst effect. Border consists of vertical lines.
Colors: pink, green, crystal, amethyst, and cobalt blue

Plate, 10" dinner, $18.

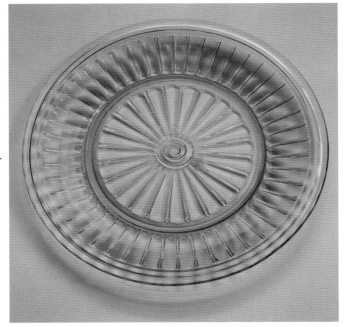

Queen Mary, "Prismatic Line," "Vertical Ribbed," Hocking Glass Co. 1936-1949. This pattern is vertically ribbed with a sunburst of radiating lines surrounded by a circular band pressed in a brilliant cast.

Colors: pink and crystal

Creamer, 5-1/2" oval, $12; Sugar, 6" oval, $12.

Plate, relish, $9.

Candy Dish with cover, $22.

Sugar, $5; Plate, 9-3/4", $18; Salt and Pepper, pair, $19; Creamer, $5.

Candlesticks, 4-1/2" double branch, single, $10 (pair, $20); Compote, 5-3/4", $15.

Ridgeleigh, Blank #1469, A. H. Heisy & Co. This pattern has deep, sharply ribbed panels that are easy to recognize.

Colors: crystal, sahara, and zircon (rare)

Sugar, $30; Creamer, $30.

17. Sandwich

This traditional American pattern in pressed glass fits into its own category due to the various companies that produced this glassware.

Sandwich – Anchor Hocking Glass Co. 1939-1964;1977. This pattern has an allover stippling spaced around flowers, foliage, and scroll motifs in an elaborate arrangement. Crimped items are common. Sandwich is a popular item and collecting is flourishing well.

Colors: desert gold (1961-1964), forest green (1956-1960s), pink (1939-1940), royal ruby (1938-1939), white/ivory or opaque (1957-1960s), and crystal.

Bowl, 8-5/8" oval, $9 in crystal.

Sugar, $9; Creamer, $8, in crystal.

Bowl, 4-7/8", $16 in red.

Sandwich, #41 – Duncan & Miller Glass Co. 1924-1955. An exquisitely decorated pattern with scrolls, foliage, diamonds, and a beaded edge.
Colors: crystal, amber, pink, green, red, and cobalt blue

Plate, 12" deviled egg, $70.

Plate, 11-1/2" handled service tray, $40.

Sandwich – Indiana Glass Co. 1920s-1980s. Pattern is not as popular due to the company reissuing their glass patterns in older glass colors and marketing them in various colors for Tiarra Home Products. The design is similar to Anchor Hocking.

Sugar and Creamer on diamond shaped tray, $16.

Colors: crystal (late 1920s-1980s), milk white (mid 1950s), amber (late 1920s-1980s), red (1933-1970), smokey blue (1976-1977), bi-centennial blue (vivid), chantilly green (light), peach, spruce, and dark green

Mayonnaise Bowl, footed, $13 in crystal.

Bowl, 8-1/2", $11 in amber.

18. Scroll

Chinex Classic, MacBeth-Evans Division of Corning Glass Works. Late 1930s-early 1940s. This pattern has an embossed scroll like design that distinguishes it from the pattern cremax.

Colors: ivory, ivory with decal decoration.

Cup, $4; Saucer, $2.

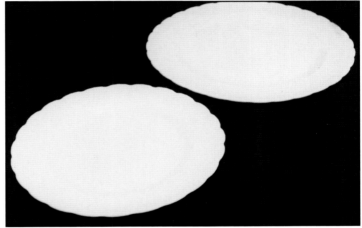

Plates, 9-3/4" dinner, $5 each.

Fire King – Soreno, Anchor Hocking Co. 1930s-1960s. Pattern has a continuous rippled scroll design in a continuing circle.

Colors: honey gold, crystal, aquamarine, green and more recent colors

Plate, dinner, $6.

Horseshoe, #612, Indiana Glass Co. 1930-1933. This pattern, especially the plate, is entirely decorated in one uninterrupted design of elaborate scroll forming a snowflake pattern.

Colors: green, yellow, pink, and crystal

Plate, 11-1/2" sandwich, $28.

Plate, 9-3/8" luncheon, $14.

Rock Crystal, "Early American Rock," McKee Glass Co. 1920s-1930s. An attractive pattern with 'S' type scrolls surrounding the five petal flower that enhances the design.

Colors: pink, green, cobalt, red, yellow, amber, blue-green, and crystal

Relish Boat, 14" six part, $50.

Plate, 8-1/2", $35 in red.

'S' Pattern, "Stippled Rose Band," MacBeth-Evans Glass Co. 1930-1933. A delicate lacy pattern, which has a circular motif in the center surrounded by an arrangement of leaves and fine stippling. Outer rim has a band of the leaf motif and stippling edged by groups of three leaves and scrolled designs. The scrolls give the pattern its name.

Colors: crystal, crystal with trims of silver, blue, green, amber, pink, fired on red, ruby, monax, and light yellow

Creamer, $7; Sugar, $6 in crystal with amber trim.

Plate, 9-1/4" dinner, $10; Plate, 8-1/4" luncheon, $6 in crystal with amber trim.

Sugar, $5; Bowl, 5-1/2", $5; Creamer, $5 in crystal.

Plate, 9-1/4" dinner, $10.

Wild Rose (with leaves and berries), Indiana Glass Co. Early 1950s-1980s. This pattern has a rose in the center with scrolls branching out into leaves with pointed edges.

Colors: multicolored, satinized, and sprayed on colors

Bowl, small, $4.

Bowl, large vegetable, $10.

Tray, two handled, $15.

19. Solids

Amethyst. A light pastel purple made by some of the companies with no definite pattern. Very popular with collectors.

Pitcher, $30.

Console Bowl, pedestal with deep scallops, $48.

Candlesticks, $20.

Black. A rich striking color, in ebony, black amethyst, and plain black. Sets in black were produced but in limited quantities. When introduced it became very popular with collectors. Some came decorated with gold, white, silver and pink, while others were just plain. A rich, striking color.

Creamer, $7; Saucer, $4; Cup, $7; Sugar, $7 (Ovide).

Bowl, 6" square handled, $20; Vase, 9-3/4" crimped top, $15; Vase, 6" two handled, $22; Compote, with decorative top, $22.

Vase, 8", $45.

Compote, 6-1/4", $35.

Sandwich Server, center
handle, $40 (Mt. Pleasant).

Blue. There are different shades of blue in the various patterns. Most popular are cobalt blue, azure blue, turquoise blue, light blues, delphite blue, and peacock blue.

Vase, in cobalt blue, $25; Vase, in amethyst, $25.

Vase, 7-1/2", $40-$45 in cobalt.

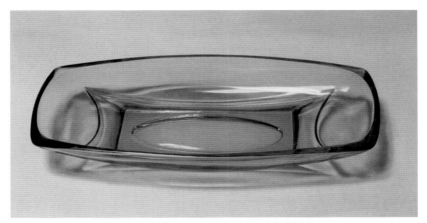

Bowl, 7-3/4" rectangular, $14 in light blue.

(L-R) Bowl, 1 pint, teardrop shape, $30; Bowl, 1 quart, teardrop shape, $35 in turquoise or robin's egg blue (Fire King).

Green. The typical Depression Glass color that's so very popular. This color has various names: emerald, springtime green, forest green, imperial green, jade, chartreuse, and opaque jade green.

Decanter, 6" round, $28; Glasses, 2 oz., $3 each in apple green.

Candlesticks, $20.

Plate, 9-1/4" dinner, square, $40; Sherbet, $8; Tumbler, $7; Cup, $6; Saucer, $2.

Bowl, $28-$30 in jadeite.

Cup and Saucer, $9; Plate, 9-1/8", $13; Bowl, 5-7/8", $20; Egg Cup, $15.

Royal Ruby. A very rich color by Anchor Hocking produced in 1938. Dinnerware is very popular with many accessory items available.

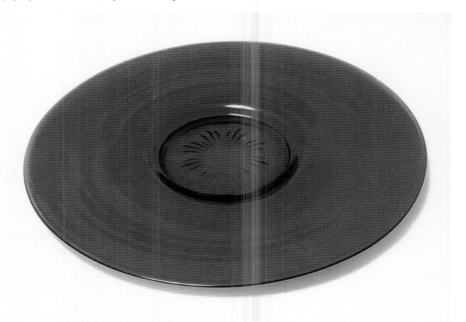

Plate, 13-3/4", $25.

Bowl, 11-1/2", $35 (scarce).

Cocktail Shaker, $50-$55 (rare).

Vase, 6-3/8", $9; Vase, 3-1/2", $6; Bowl, 6-3/4" footed bon bon, $15; Relish Dish, handled, $7-$12.

20. Squares

Capri, Hazel Ware Division of Continental Can. 1960s. Refers to the color blue rather than an actual pattern name. Square pieces are called "Colony."

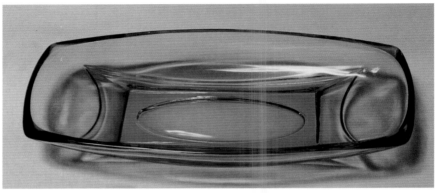

Bowl, 7-3/4" rectangular, with a square base, $14.

Bowl, 5-3/4" deep square, $10.

Moroccan Amethyst, Hazel Ware Division of Continental Can. 1960s. This is the rich purple color with the square based pieces being called "Colony" as they are in "Capri." a rich blue coloring made also by Hazel Ware.

Colors: amethyst

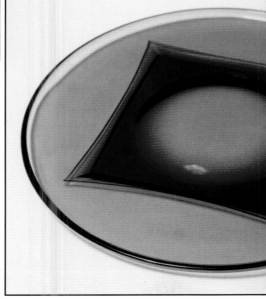

Plate, 12" round, with square base, $15.

Bowl, rectangular, with square base and metal handle, $18; Bowl, 5-3/4" – 6" round, with square base, $12.

Chip and Dip, 10-3/4" and 5-3/4" bowls, with metal holder, $40; Plate, 12" round, with square base, $15.

21. Swirls

Capri, "Seashell," Hazel Ware Division of Continental Can. 1960s. Pattern consists of large "seashell" shaped swirls.

  Colors: azure blue

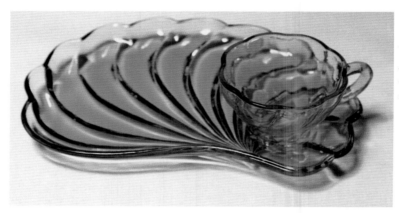

Snack Set: Plate, 10" fan shaped with cup rest, $9; Cup, round swirled, $5.

Caprice, Cambridge Glass Co. 1940s-1957. An elegant pattern that has the distinct, deep swirls that are so easy to detect.

  Colors: crystal, moonlight blue, blue, amber, amethyst, la rosa, dark emerald green, pistachio ritz blue, and milk glass

Pitcher, 80 oz ball shape, $335.

Candlesticks, 7" with prism, $75 each.

Colony, Line #412, Fostoria Glass Co. 1920s-1980s. This pattern is very distinctive with its swirled lines, ribbed edges, and beaded bottom.

Colors: crystal, some yellow, blue, green, white, amber, red (1980s – Maypole)

Candy Dish, 6-1/2" with cover, $45.

Bowl, 5" handled, $15.

Diana, Federal Glass Co. 1937-1941. A simple pattern of fine swirled lines leading out from the center of the plates and wide rims of slightly larger radial curved lines. Colors: pink, amber, and crystal

Bowl, 9" salad, $22.

Plate, 11-3/4" sandwich with gold trim, $10; Cup, $6; Saucer, $3.

Bowl, 9" salad, $18; Plate, 11-3/4" sandwich, $10 in amber.

Plate, 9 1/2", $9; Cup, $9; Saucer, $2.

Fire King – "Swirl," Anchor Hocking Glass Corp. 1950s. This pattern consists of anchor white swirls with the gold trim or border, and was primarily considered dinnerware.

Colors: azurite, ivory, ivory trimmed in gold or red, white or white trimmed in gold or red, and pink

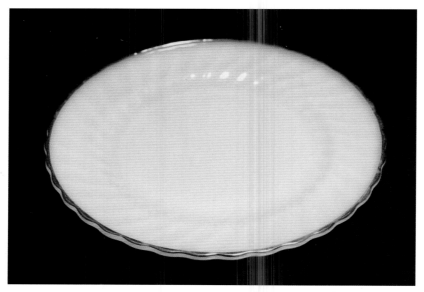

Plate, 9-1/8" dinner, $10.

Moroccan Amethyst, Hazel Ware Division of Continental Can. 1960s. This has a distinct swirled design in the rich purple color.

Colors: amethyst

Candy Dish, with tall lid, $38.

Spiral, Hocking Glass Co. 1928-1930. A swirled pattern with the swirls going to the left or clockwise, distinguishing this pattern from "Twisted Optic."
Colors: green, crystal, and pink

Preserve, with cover, $35.

Sherbet, $5 each.

Swirl, "Petal Swirl," Jeannette Glass Co. 1937-1938. Pattern has a motif of concentric ribbed circles and an outer rim of swirled ribs on the border.
Colors: pink, green, amber, some blue, and some canary yellow

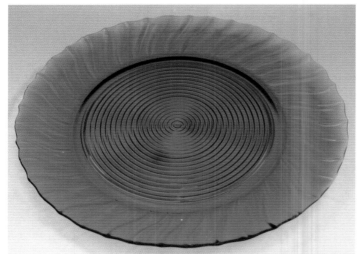

Plate, 12-1/2" sandwich, $32.

Sugar, $22, Bowl, $16; Creamer, $18.

Candy Dish, open three legged, $15 in pink.

156

Twisted Optic, Imperial Glass Co. 1927-1930. This is a twisted pattern of swirls or spirals that go in the direction of right or counterclockwise.

Colors: pink, green, amber, some blue, and canary yellow

Plate, 8" luncheon, $6.

Cup, $4; Saucer, $2; Plate, luncheon, $6.

Waverly, A.H. Heisy and Co. A crystal pattern with a swirled or waved design.
Colors: crystal, amber (rare)

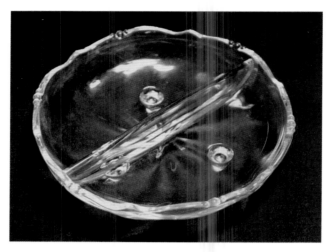

Cheese Dish, 5-1/2" footed, $20.

Wild Rose, Jeannette Glass Co. 1939. Pattern is typical of the swirl look, with numerous swirled panels.
Colors: royal ruby

Pitcher, 80 oz., titled, $60.

Bibliography

Bredehoft, Tom and Neila. *Fifty Years of Collecting Glass, 1920-1970*. Iola, WI: Krause Publications, 2000.

Brenner, Robert. *Depression Glass for Collectors*. Atglen, PA: Schiffer Publishing, Ltd., 1998.

Florence, Gene. *Glass Pattern Identification Guide*. Paducah, KY: Collector Books, 1998.

———. *Collectors Encyclopedia of Depression Glass*. Paducah, KY: Collector Books, 2001.

———. *Elegant Glassware of the Depression Era*. Paducah, KY: Collector Books, 2001.

———. *Collectible Glassware of the 40's, 50's, 60's*. Paducah, KY: Collector Books, 2002.

Kovel, Ralph and Terry. *Depression Glass and American Dinnerware*. New York, NY: Crown Publishers, 1991.

Mauzy, Barbara. *Mauzy's Comprehensive Handbook of Depression Glass Prices*. Atglen, PA: Schiffer Publishing, Ltd., 2001.

Rinker, Harry L. *Warmen's Antiques and their Prices*. Radnor, PA: Wallace-Homestead Book Co., 1995.

Weatherman, Hazel. *Colored Glassware of the Depression Era Vol. 1*. Ozark, Missouri: Weatherman Glass Books, 1970.

———. *Colored Glassware of the Depression Era Vol. 2*. Ozark, Missouri: Weatherman Glass Books, 1974.

Yeske, Doris. *Depression Glass: A Collector's Guide. Revised 5th Edtion*. Atglen, PA: Schiffer Publishing, Ltd., 2001.

———. *Depression Glass: Collections and Reflections. Revised & Expanded 2nd Edition*. Atglen, PA: Schiffer Publishing, Ltd., 2002.

Index